It is the soul,
and not the strong-box,
which should be filled.

— SENECA

Blue Mountain Arts.

Bestselling Titles

By Susan Polis Schutz:
To My Daughter with Love on the Important Things in Life
To My Son with Love

By Douglas Pagels:
30 Beautiful Things That Are True About You
42 Gifts I'd Like to Give to You
100 Things to Always Remember... and One Thing to Never Forget
May You Always Have an Angel by Your Side
To the One Person I Consider to Be My Soul Mate

By Donna Fargo:
I Prayed for You Today
To the Love of My Life

52 Lessons on Communicating Love
by Dr. Ruth Westheimer

Is It Time to Make a Change?
by Deanna Beisser

Anthologies:
7 Days to a Positive Attitude
Always Believe in Yourself and Your Dreams
For You, My Daughter
Friends for Life
Hang In There
I Love You, Mom
I'm Glad You Are My Sister
The Joys and Challenges of Motherhood
The Language of Recovery
Marriage Is a Promise of Love
Teaching and Learning Are Lifelong Journeys
There Is Greatness Within You, My Son
Think Positive Thoughts Every Day
Thoughts to Share with a Wonderful Teenager
True Wealth
With God by Your Side ...You Never Have to Be Alone
You're Just like a Sister to Me

The Secrets to a Soulful Life

How to Create Peace and Happiness in Your Life Every Day

Edited by Patricia Wayant

Blue Mountain Press ®

Boulder, Colorado

ACKNOWLEDGMENTS

We gratefully acknowledge the permission granted by the following authors, publishers, and authors' representatives to reprint poems or excerpts from their publications.

Wally Amos for "Bring forth the best...." Copyright © 2006 by Wally Amos. All rights reserved.

HarperCollins Publishers for "Accomplishing your daily goals..." from CREATING A CHARMED LIFE by Victoria Moran. Copyright © 1999 by Victoria Moran. All rights reserved. And for "Soak up the love..." and "Fall in love with..." from JOURNEY TO THE HEART: DAILY MEDITATIONS ON THE PATH TO FREEING YOUR SOUL by Melody Beattie. Copyright © 1996 by Melody Beattie. All rights reserved. And for "A smile costs nothing..." from MAKE YOUR LIFE WORTH WHILE by Emmet Fox. Copyright 1942, 1943, 1944, 1945, 1946 by Emmet Fox. Copyright renewed © 1974 by Kathleen Whelan. All rights reserved. And for "Life is not a single..." from PULLING YOUR OWN STRINGS by Dr. Wayne W. Dyer. Copyright © 1991 by Wayne W. Dyer. All rights reserved. And for "The purpose of life, after all..." from YOU LEARN BY LIVING by Eleanor Roosevelt. Copyright © 1960 by Eleanor Roosevelt. All rights reserved. And for "Work affects the soul..." from CARE OF THE SOUL by Thomas Moore. Copyright © 1992 by Thomas Moore. All rights reserved.

Vintage Books, a division of Random House, Inc., for "There is a miracle that happens..." from LETTERS TO A YOUNG POET by Rainer Maria Rilke, translated by Stephen Mitchell. Copyright © 1984 by Stephen Mitchell. All rights reserved.

Doubleday, a division of Random House, Inc., for "The past drags behind us..." and "Begin trusting your own sense..." from NOTES ON HOW TO LIVE IN THE WORLD... AND STILL BE HAPPY by Hugh Prather. Copyright © 1986 by Hugh Prather. All rights reserved. And for "Follow your bliss and..." from THE POWER OF MYTH by Joseph Campbell. Copyright © 1988 by Apostrophe S Productions, Inc., and Alfred van der Marck Editions. All rights reserved.

Dana Curtin for "There's a joy in the small things...." Copyright © 2006 by Dana Curtin. All rights reserved.

Christine Hope Starr for "To forgive is not to forget." Copyright © 2006 by Christine Hope Starr. All rights reserved.

St. Martin's Press for "Beyond your challenges...," "Living a passionate and awakened...," and "Living with authenticity" from HOW DID I GET HERE? by Barbara De Angelis, PhD. Copyright © 2005 by Barbara De Angelis, PhD. All rights reserved.

CMG and the Frank Lloyd Wright Foundation for "The longer I live the more..." by Frank Lloyd Wright. Copyright © by the Frank Lloyd Wright Foundation. All rights reserved.

(Acknowledgments continued on page 64)

We wish to thank Susan Polis Schutz for permission to reprint the following quotes in this publication: "Nature is the most peaceful..." and "You have to find a way...." Copyright © 2004 by Stephen Schutz and Susan Polis Schutz. All rights reserved.

Library of Congress Control Number: 2006902018
ISBN-13: 978-1-59842-169-9
ISBN-10: 1-59842-169-7

Certain trademarks are used under license.
BLUE MOUNTAIN PRESS is registered in U.S. Patent and Trademark Office.

Printed in the United States of America.
First Printing: 2006

 This book is printed on recycled paper.

This book is printed on fine quality, laid embossed, 80 lb. paper. This paper has been specially produced to be acid free (neutral pH) and contains no groundwood or unbleached pulp. It conforms with all the requirements of the American National Standards Institute, Inc., so as to ensure that this book will last and be enjoyed by future generations.

Blue Mountain Arts, Inc.
P.O. Box 4549, Boulder, Colorado 80306

CONTENTS

Introduction 7
Make the Most of Each Day 9
Give Your Best to the World 10
Take Time for the People Who Matter Most 11
Live in a Spirit of Love 13
Let Go of the Past 14
Find Your Joy 15
Be Grateful 17
Forgive 18
Show Kindness 19
Know Yourself 21
Never Lose Sight of What's Beautiful 22
Take Nothing for Granted 23
Walk Your Spiritual Path 25
Realize Your Oneness with the Universe 26
Spend Time in Nature 27
Be Compassionate Toward Others 29
Rid Your Life of Worry and Stress 30
Live in a State of Grace 31
Simplify 33
Slow Down 34
Let Yourself Relax 35
Find Something to Be Passionate About 37
Accept That Nothing Is Ever Perfect 38
Resolve Any Conflicts 39
Take Good Care of Yourself 41
Let Nothing Disturb Your Peace of Mind 42
Be Alone Sometimes 43
Live Authentically 45
Look for Reasons to Smile 46
Never Stop Growing 47
Do Good Work 49
Fill Your Mind with Positive Thoughts 50
Keep Your Sense of Wonder 51
Recognize Beginnings and Endings 53
Welcome Change 54
Cultivate Community 55
Value Time 57
Share Yourself with Those You Love 58
Be in the Present 59
Love and Honor Yourself 61
May You Have a Soulful Life 62

INTRODUCTION

To LIVE a soulful life is to feel a profound connection to everyone and everything that touches your life. It is to go about your day with greater awareness of the world around you and to live with love and gratitude in your heart. To live a soulful life is to tap into the deepest, richest place inside you to find your true self, to realize your life purpose, and to experience life in the most positive ways.

People who live soulful lives embrace every moment they are given. They cherish the people, places, and things that fill their lives with so much warmth and joy. They take time when others around them are rushing and feel intensely when it would be easier not to feel at all. They know things go wrong, mistakes get made, and bad stuff happens, but they try to focus on the beauty and goodness in the world. They recognize that each new day is a gift that will never come again.

There is no single definition of soulful living and the secrets to finding it can really only be found inside yourself. Whether you are just starting down the path to discovering what a soulful life is for you or you desire to bring more depth and meaning to the road you're already on, the quotes and writings in this book are simply a place to begin. Hopefully, they will provide the inspiration you need to achieve greater peace and happiness in your life.

MAKE THE MOST OF EACH DAY

Don't just have minutes in the day, have moments in time. Balance out any bad with the good you can provide. Know that you are capable of amazing results. Surprise yourself by discovering new strength inside.

Add a meaningful page to the diary of each day. Do things no one else would even dream of. There is no greater gift than the kind of inner beauty you possess. Do the things you do... with love.

Walk along the pathways that enrich your happiness. Taking care of the "little things" is a big necessity. Don't be afraid of testing your courage. Life is short, but it's long enough to have excitement and serenity.

Don't let the important things go unsaid. Do the things that brighten your life and help you on your way. Live to the fullest; make each day count.

— COLLIN MCCARTY

GIVE YOUR BEST
TO THE WORLD

Bring forth the best in everything you touch and everyone
you meet, and you in turn will become better and better.
Everyone's life will be constantly enriched from within and
without; the world will be better because you are here.

— WALLY AMOS

Choose to do the things that will reflect well... on
your ability, your integrity, your spirit, your health,
your tomorrows, your smiles, your dreams, and yourself.

— DOUGLAS PAGELS

Follow your feelings and consider them to
be the voice of your innermost beliefs.

— GEORGE SAND

TAKE TIME FOR THE PEOPLE WHO MATTER MOST

In our busy lives, we often forget that there is more along the way than just bills to pay, phone calls to return, and errands to run. There are people in our lives who need to be hugged, who need to be loved. There are people in our lives who need their accomplishments noticed and praised... We need to remember that a heart is like a garden that needs to be tended to and nourished with what only another heart can give — love and appreciation, devotion and honesty.

— TRACIA GLOUDEMANS

Fill your heart with the kindness of friends, the caring of everyone you love, and the richness of memories you wouldn't trade for anything.

— DOUGLAS PAGELS

TO LIVE A SOULFUL LIFE IS TO...

LIVE IN A SPIRIT OF LOVE

You will find as you look back upon your life
that the moments that stand out, the moments
when you have really lived, are the moments
when you have done things in a spirit of love.

— HENRY DRUMMOND

Accomplishing your daily goals has a place, but the
heart has a valid agenda of its own. When you can look
back on a day and find within it even one warm memory
or a single touching story, you've paid attention to your
heart. That's worth whatever time it took.

— VICTORIA MORAN

There is a miracle that happens every time to those who
really love: the more they give, the more they possess of
that precious nourishing love from which flowers and
children have their strength.

— RAINER MARIA RILKE

LET GO OF THE PAST

There's nothing wrong with
thinking back; but it probably is
a mistake to dwell on
the past "what if's."
Instead, we should concentrate
on today, on tomorrow,
and on the tomorrows yet to be.

— LAUREL ATHERTON

The past drags behind us like an endless string of
junk tied to a wedding car. It may sound unusual
and attract attention, but in not cutting it loose
we are drowning out the gentle music we long to
hear. Do not pull the past into the present. In the
present you are free. Merely leave behind all that
is behind, and know the lightness, the happiness,
this little practice can bring.

— HUGH PRATHER

FIND YOUR JOY

There's joy in the small things — a cat softly curled in the morning sun, a child's hand sweetly holding yours, the note on the fridge that says "I love you," your favorite song on the way to work, a single flower left on your desk, a warm comforter on a winter's night, the smell of hot chocolate in the morning mountain air, fresh sheets, clean towels, a daffodil peeking timidly from the soil, a friend's embrace when all seems lost, the newborn sun day in, day out.

There's joy in the small things. Sit for a quiet moment, and hear the still, small voice of joy within you.

— DANA CURTIN

Happiness resides not in possessions and not in gold, the feeling of happiness dwells in the soul.

— DEMOCRITUS

Joy is not in things; it is in us.

— RICHARD WAGNER

BE GRATEFUL

"Gratitude" is one of the nicest feelings a heart can have. It's a feeling that comes along for a very special reason — and it's a lovely thought that never goes away once it enters in. It joins together with precious memories and grateful hopes. Gratitude lives on, not for just a moment or a day, but through all the seasons that lie ahead.

— MARIN MCKAY

If we knew how much the habit of being thankful might do for us, I am sure we would take time out every day to count up a few of our blessings. When the spirit of thankfulness takes its place in our consciousness, we radiate life from the very center of our being to the world about us.

— AUTHOR UNKNOWN

There is always something for which to be thankful.

— CHARLES DICKENS

FORGIVE

To forgive is not to forget
It really is to remember that nobody is perfect
That each of us stumbles
When we want so much to stay upright
That each of us says things we wish we had never said
That we can all forget that love
Is more important than being right
To forgive is really to remember
That we are so much more than our mistakes
That we are more often kind and caring
That accepting another's flaws
Can help us accept our own
To forgive is to remember the odds are pretty good
That we might soon need to be forgiven ourselves
That life sometimes gives us more
Than we can handle gracefully
To forgive is to remember
That we have room in our hearts to begin again

— CHRISTINE HOPE STARR

SHOW KINDNESS

Soak up the love and warmth from the world around you.
Take that warmth into your everyday life. Open your heart
more to the people you see, the people you meet, the
people you greet, and the people you love. Practice being
warm, loving, and open. Do more than just think a kind
loving thought. Say it. Do more than just think of something
nice you'd like to do for someone. Do it.

— MELODY BEATTIE

Life is made up, not of great sacrifices or duties, but
of little things in which smiles and kindness and small
obligations, given habitually, are what win and preserve
the heart and secure comfort.

— SIR HUMPHREY DAVY

Little acts of kindness are stowed away in
the heart like bags of lavender in a drawer,
to sweeten every object around them.

— AUTHOR UNKNOWN

KNOW YOURSELF

Beyond your challenges, beyond your successes, beyond the events with which life has molded your spirit, there is a placeless place within you. It is a place of peace. It is a place of freedom. It is the place where the Self you have been seeking resides.

— BARBARA DE ANGELIS, PHD

Begin trusting your own sense of happiness, of what makes you happy and what does not. Let it spread to your diet, your clothes, your relationships, your spiritual yearnings. Let it infuse your spending and saving, your health and your habitat. Sit down often and know your own heart.

— HUGH PRATHER

Without knowing what I am and why I am here, life is impossible.

— LEO TOLSTOY

NEVER LOSE SIGHT OF WHAT'S BEAUTIFUL

Half the joy of life is in little things taken on the run. Let us run if we must — even the sands do that — but let us keep our hearts young and our eyes open that nothing worth our while shall escape us.

— VICTOR CHERBULIEZ

Beauty can be discovered in so many surprising places. It is in the warmth of a sincere smile, in the sparkle that lights up the eyes of someone special, in the setting sun, in the autumn leaves as they float among the trees. And inside the heart, soul, and mind is a beauty that can't be described.

— REGINA HILL

The longer I live the more beautiful life becomes. If you foolishly ignore beauty, you will soon find yourself without it. Your life will be impoverished. But if you invest in beauty, it will remain with you all the days of your life.

— FRANK LLOYD WRIGHT

TAKE NOTHING
FOR GRANTED

Take nothing for granted: the sheer act
of waking each day; fresh air upon your cheek;
each effort expended on self or another —
walking the dog, shopping for food,
toiling at home, in an office, or on the road.
Every moment is rare, short, and full of glory.
Every word is magic;
a story achieved through will.
Marvel at nature's moods as mirror of your own.
Recall a sunrise or sunset,
a flock of geese in the sky.
Care about parents or children as fragile gifts,
like petals on a rose, like songs from one bird.
Praise the simple or complex —
the invention of flight above clouds;
the wheel; the bathtub; a rocking chair.
We rise and fall in the moon or a wave,
in a smile or many tears.
And being brave is to be alive
as we give and share love always,
only and ever to survive.

— ROCHELLE LYNN HOLT

WALK YOUR SPIRITUAL PATH

Every now and again take a good look at something not made with hands — a mountain, a star, the turn of a stream. There will come to you wisdom and patience and solace and, above all, the assurance that you are not alone in the world.

— SIDNEY LOVETT

What does the word "soul" mean?... No one can give a definition of the soul. But we know what it feels like. The soul is the sense of something higher than ourselves, something that stirs in us thoughts, hopes, and aspirations which go out to the world of goodness, truth, and beauty.

— ALBERT SCHWEITZER

The spiritual dimension is your core, your center, your commitment to your value system. It's a very private area of life and a supremely important one. It draws upon the sources that inspire and uplift you and tie you to the timeless truths of all humanity.

— STEPHEN R. COVEY

REALIZE YOUR ONENESS WITH THE UNIVERSE

The first peace, which is the most important, is that which comes within the souls of people when they realize their oneness with the universe and all its powers.

— BLACK ELK

Live as well as you know how in all the spheres of life. Live well in your mind, think rich thoughts, be curious, be mentally alive. Live well with others. Enjoy them, love people, try to help when you can and leave people alone when that seems best. Live well physically. Take care of your body and your health. Live well culturally, with time for nature, paintings, poetry, and music. Live well spiritually. Realize your oneness with the universe and with the Infinite. Two words say it all, in every way, live well.

— WILFERD A. PETERSON

SPEND TIME IN NATURE

Go for a walk and stop to notice the trees, flowers, and wildlife you pass. Visit an indoor garden in a shopping mall or conservatory and inhale the green scents. Watch a babbling brook, or waves breaking on a beach, and lose yourself in the sounds — or lie in the grass and look up and watch the clouds float by. If you're in the city, you can re-create the beauty of nature by visiting a botanical garden, buying yourself some flowers or a plant (or just browsing at a flower shop). This escape to the natural world will give you some distance from your everyday cares and help you put them in perspective. Seeing that the world goes on as always, in its soothing, harmonic rhythms, can restore you.

— SARAH, THE DUCHESS OF YORK

Nature is the most peaceful environment for clarifying your thoughts and putting things into perspective.

— SUSAN POLIS SCHUTZ

BE COMPASSIONATE TOWARD OTHERS

Compassion is the act of opening your heart. To live in a state of compassion means you approach the world with your emotional barriers lowered and your ability to connect with others intact. Compassion is the emotional glue that keeps you rooted in the universality of the human experience, as it connects you to your essence and to the essence of those around you.

— CHÉRIE CARTER-SCOTT, PHD

We do not exist for ourselves alone, and it is only when we are fully convinced of this fact that we begin to love ourselves properly and thus also love others. What do I mean by loving ourselves properly? I mean, first of all, desiring to live, accepting life as a very great gift and a great good, not because of what it gives us, but because of what it enables us to give others.

— THOMAS MERTON

The most priceless gifts we can give to each other are the understanding and caring that come from the heart. And each and every one of us has these gifts to offer... through the gift of ourselves.

— BEN DANIELS

RID YOUR LIFE OF WORRY AND STRESS

You have to find a way to balance your work, private
life, and everything else that is important to you.

— SUSAN POLIS SCHUTZ

Do not anticipate trouble,
or worry about what may never happen.
Keep in the sunlight.

— BENJAMIN FRANKLIN

If you want to be healthy morally, mentally, and physically,
just let go. Let go of the little annoyances of everyday life,
the irritations and the petty vexations that cross your path
daily. Don't take them up, nurse them, pet them, and brood
over them. They are not worthwhile. Let them go!

Learn to let go. As you value health of body and peace of
mind, let go — just simply let go!

— AUTHOR UNKNOWN

LIVE IN A STATE OF GRACE

To live in a state of grace means to be fully in tune with your spiritual nature and a higher power that sustains you. Grace comes when you are able to move from your lower self, where your ego dictates the path that "should be" rightfully yours, to your higher self, where you are able to transcend your ego and expand into your greater good. It comes when you shift from a "me"-centered reality to an understanding of the bigger picture. Grace comes when you understand and accept that the universe always creates circumstances that lead every person to his or her own true path, and that everything happens for a reason as part of a divine plan....

In the state of grace you trust in yourself and the universe. You can celebrate other people's blessings, knowing that their gifts are right and appropriate for them and that the universe has your gift right around the corner.

— CHÉRIE CARTER-SCOTT, PHD

The winds of grace are always blowing.
It is you that must raise your sails.

— RABINDRANATH TAGORE

SIMPLIFY

Human beings are full of desires. Day and night, they run after these desires, and therefore they are not free. If they are not free, they do not feel at ease and they do not feel happy. If we have few desires, we are satisfied with a simple, wholesome life and we have the time to live deeply every moment of daily life and to love and look after our dear ones. That is the secret of true happiness.

— THICH NHAT HANH

As you begin to live more seriously within, you begin to live more simply without.

— RALPH WALDO EMERSON

Simplicity is not a matter of time management or efficiency or organization. It does not consist of shedding one set of life furnishings in order to make room for another. Rather, a simpler life is one in which the knowledge of what matters dictates all that surrounds us. It is a life lived with the courage to let go of what our hearts know does not belong. It is a more balanced life, not a more expert balancing act.

— ANDREA VAN STEENHOUSE, PHD

SLOW DOWN

Be at peace with all that life brings.
Be at rest in your soul.

— H. DRESSER

It's useful to get things done in a timely manner. And yet, the quickest way is not always the best way.

Our culture has become geared to immediate gratification. But often, life's treasures can gain much more value when you wait awhile for them.

Though there are more and more ways to achieve instant results, there is really no way to receive instant fulfillment. The things that bring real meaning and joy to life are the things in which you're able to invest yourself over time.

Life is best when it can be savored. Rushing from one thing to the next can fill your days with sensation, yet it leaves your spirit sadly empty.

You don't have to do it all or have it all today. Take the time to fully experience and enjoy the moment you're in.

Life is already filled with more richness than you could ever imagine. Give yourself the opportunity to take it all in.

— RALPH MARSTON

LET YOURSELF RELAX

We are too busy with career, business, dropping off the kids, meetings, hairdressers, groceries, dry cleaners, and talking on the phone to put aside time each day to relax our minds.... It is essential to our spirituality to have time to think about those things that matter. Without it, it is impossible to grow spiritually and emotionally.

— SUZANNE SOMERS

One should clean out a room in one's home and place only a tea table and a chair in the room with some boiled water and fragrant tea. Afterwards, sit salutarily and allow one's spirit to become tranquil, light, and natural.

— LI RI HUA

Rest is not idleness, and to lie sometimes on the grass under trees on a summer's day, listening to the murmur of the water, or watching the clouds float across the sky, is by no means a waste of time.

— SIR J. LUBBOCK

FIND SOMETHING TO BE PASSIONATE ABOUT

Living a passionate and awakened life means looking at the stars each night as if it were your first time and as if it were your last time. It means embracing your loved ones as if this were the only embrace you will ever be granted. It means living each day with reverence and wonder as if it were the only day you will be given to live.

— BARBARA DE ANGELIS, PHD

Follow your bliss and don't be afraid, and doors will open where you didn't know they were going to be.

— JOSEPH CAMPBELL

The purpose of life, after all, is to live it, to taste experience to the utmost, to reach out eagerly and without fear for newer and richer experience.

— ELEANOR ROOSEVELT

ACCEPT THAT NOTHING IS EVER PERFECT

Some days, doing "the best we can" may still fall short of what we would like to be able to do, but life isn't perfect — on any front — and doing what we can with what we have is the most we should expect of ourselves or anyone else.

— FRED ROGERS

Perfectionism is not a quest for the best. It is a pursuit of the worst in ourselves, the part that tells us that nothing we do will ever be good enough — that we should try again.

— JULIA CAMERON

Do not let trifles disturb your tranquility of mind.... Life is too precious to be sacrificed for the nonessential and transient.... Ignore the inconsequential.

— GRENVILLE KLEISER

RESOLVE ANY CONFLICTS

If you're harboring the slightest bitterness toward anyone, or any unkind thoughts of any sort whatever, you must get rid of them quickly. They are not hurting anyone but you. It isn't enough just to do right things and say right things — you must also *think* right things before your life can come into harmony.

— PEACE PILGRIM

Resentment always hurts you more than it does the person you resent. While your offender has probably forgotten the offense and gone on with life, you continue to stew in your pain, perpetuating the past.

— RICK WARREN

If we don't forgive ourselves for our mistakes, and others for the wounds they have inflicted upon us, we end up crippled with guilt. And the soul cannot grow under a blanket of guilt, because guilt is isolating, while growth is a gradual process of reconnection to ourselves, to other people, and to a larger whole.

— JOAN BORYSENKO, PHD

TAKE GOOD CARE OF YOURSELF

Care enough about yourself to eat right, get enough exercise and rest, and not do anything that would cause you harm, now or in the future.

Have someone to confide in, laugh with, and explore new things with; someone who is a great listener.

Always have confidence in yourself, your talents, your abilities, and your uniqueness. Believe that you are a likable and desirable person who deserves respect and consideration.

— BARBARA CAGE

Fall in love with yourself. Be gentle, loving, kind, and attentive. Take time throughout each day to tend to your needs, just as you would tend to someone you loved deeply and dearly.

— MELODY BEATTIE

LET NOTHING DISTURB YOUR PEACE OF MIND

Be so strong that nothing can disturb your peace of mind. Talk health, happiness, and prosperity to every person you meet. Make all your friends feel there is something in them. Look at the sunny side of everything. Think only of the best, work only for the best, and expect only the best. Be as enthusiastic about the success of others as you are about your own. Forget the mistakes of the past and press on to the greater achievements of the future. Give everyone a smile. Spend so much time improving yourself that you have no time left to criticize others. Be too big for worry and too noble for anger.

— CHRISTIAN D. LARSEN

Even if I knew that tomorrow the world would go to pieces, I would still plant my apple tree.

— MARTIN LUTHER

BE ALONE SOMETIMES

When one is a stranger to oneself then one is estranged from others too. If one is out of touch with oneself, then one cannot touch others. How often in a large city, shaking hands with my friends, I have felt the wilderness stretching between us. Both of us were wandering in arid wastes, having lost the springs that nourished us — or having found them dry. Only when one is connected to one's own core is one connected to others, I am beginning to discover. And, for me, the core, the inner spring, can best be refound through solitude.

— ANNE MORROW LINDBERGH

Remember that being alone
doesn't always mean being lonely;
it can be a beautiful experience
of finding your creativity,
your heartfelt feelings,
and the calm and quiet peace deep inside you.

— JACQUELINE SCHIFF

LIVE AUTHENTICALLY

Living with authenticity means that who you appear to be to others is who you really are. Your beliefs, your values, your commitments, your inner realities are all reflected in how you live your life on the outside. The more you live authentically, as who you truly are, the more peace you will experience.

— BARBARA DE ANGELIS, PHD

Living authentically is what you're doing when you find congruence between your inner world — your feelings, values, gifts, needs, spirituality, and passions — and your outer world — your job, relationships, home, and community. When you live your authentic life, these things support and synergize each other. It doesn't mean that you have no worries, conflicts, or fears; you may even have more as you choose to live authentically. There is one key difference, though: they no longer have the power to unseat you. When you have discovered what you can offer to others, when you feel that you are on your unique path, when you have an ongoing, honest, reliable connection to your inner wisdom, then you have found your unique spot in this world with all its craziness, sorrow, and joy.

— SUSAN PIVER

LOOK FOR REASONS TO SMILE

Spend awhile in the garden or the park or the path amongst the trees. Do the things that please you, as well as the things you have to do. Fulfill the work and the tasks of the day while discovering something new and different along the way. Grow, learn, reach out. Be curious. Be childlike.

Remember what imagination is all about. Share a smile, a feeling, a certain personal thought from the heart, from the soul. Care. Kick off your shoes. Sing along with your song. Be less concerned about what others think of you. Be more accepting of the very special person who lives inside you.

— COLLIN MCCARTY

A smile costs nothing in money, time, or effort, but it is literally true that it can be of supreme importance in one's life.

— EMMET FOX

NEVER STOP GROWING

When you think you know it all, then you deny yourself the opportunity to learn anything new. When you decide that you've seen it all, you cut yourself off from new and enlightening experiences.

Every day is an opportunity to grow. Always take advantage of that opportunity, for it is a big part of what makes you alive.

No matter how much you've already accomplished, you can still receive great benefit from new challenges. No matter what your level of learning and experience, you can always raise that level even higher.

When you think you have all the answers, get busy and find some more questions. View each new discovery as a starting point and not as a final destination.

The joy of life is in the journey. The fulfillment of life is in the growing. Keep that growing going, and never let it stop.

— RALPH MARSTON

You nourish your soul by fulfilling your destiny, by developing the potential that the soul represents.

— RABBI HAROLD KUSHNER

DO GOOD WORK

Work affects the soul profoundly. It is full of imagination and speaks to the soul at many different levels. It may, for example, conjure up certain memories and fantasies that have special significance. These may be connected to family myths, traditions, and ideals. Or work may be a means of sorting out issues that have little to do with the work itself. It may be a response to fate. We may find ourselves doing work that has been in the family for generations or working at a job that appeared after a number of coincidences and chance events. In this sense, all work is a vocation, a calling from a place that is the source of meaning and identity, the roots of which lie beyond human intention and interpretation.

— THOMAS MOORE

Who are the happiest people on earth? A craftsman or artist whistling over a job well done. A little child building sand castles. A mother, after a busy day, bathing her baby. A doctor who has finished a difficult and dangerous operation and saved a human life. Happiness lies in a constructive job well done.

Get your happiness out of your work or you will never know what happiness is.

— ELBERT HUBBARD

FILL YOUR MIND WITH POSITIVE THOUGHTS

Always think on the bright side —
no matter what life brings to your day.
You'll gain a treasure within your soul
that no worry or hardship can ever take away.

— ISAAC PURCELL

Seek out that particular mental attribute which makes you
feel most deeply and vitally alive, along with which comes
the inner voice which says, "This is the real me," and when
you have found that attitude, follow it.

— WILLIAM JAMES

The pleasantest things in the world are
pleasant thoughts: and the great art of
life is to have as many of them as possible.

— MICHEL DE MONTAIGNE

KEEP YOUR SENSE OF WONDER

Every hour of the day and night is an
unspeakably perfect miracle.

— WALT WHITMAN

I have never known an "interesting" person who was not
passionately interested in so many things that it was a wonder
how he ever got around to them, and who did not take an
excited interest in all those commonplace little things in life
which most of us find so deadly dull. Like children, they can't
pass a flower without wanting to smell it, see a boat in dock
without wanting to know when it sails and for what port,
pass a hole in the ground without wanting to get down in
there and investigate. They are filled to the teeth with
questions they must answer before they die. They have never
lost their sense of wonder.

— MARIE BEYNON RAY

Every morning, wake with the awe of just being alive.
Each day, discover the magnificent, awesome beauty
in the world. Explore and embrace life in yourself and
in everyone you see each day.

— VICKIE M. WORSHAM

RECOGNIZE BEGINNINGS AND ENDINGS

For a long time it had seemed to me that life was about to begin — real life. But there was always some obstacle in the way, something to be got through first, some unfinished business, time still to be served.... Then life would begin. At last it dawned on me that these obstacles were my life.

— FR. ALFRED D'SOUZA

Every day is a fresh beginning.
Every morn is the world made new.

— SUSAN COOLIDGE

Sometimes you're just done and you know it. You're finished. It's time to turn the page and get on to the next chapter. It's as if you've grown too large for your own story and you're bursting at all kinds of seams. It's time for the next phase, time to begin a new cycle. There's nothing wrong. It's not a problem. You've simply completed whatever you set out to do. Embrace your endings and honor the fullness of completion. Then you can move with grace and ease into the brand-new beginnings that await you.

— RACHEL SNYDER

WELCOME CHANGE

Life is not a single experience. Life is always changing, and every day of your life — every moment of every day — represents something totally new, which has never existed before, and which can be used in uncountable new ways if you decide to view it that way.

— DR. WAYNE W. DYER

We must always change, renew, rejuvenate ourselves; otherwise we harden.

— JOHANN WOLFGANG VON GOETHE

Everything in life that we really accept undergoes a change.

— KATHERINE MANSFIELD

CULTIVATE COMMUNITY

Inner peace comes through working for the good of all. We are all cells in the body of humanity — all of us, all over the world. Each one has a contribution to make, and will know from within what this contribution is, but no one can find inner peace except by working, not in a self-centered way, but for the whole human family.

— PEACE PILGRIM

No man is an island of itself. Each is a piece of the continent, a part of the main.

— JOHN DONNE

One great, strong, unselfish soul in every community would actually redeem the world.

— ELBERT HUBBARD

It is one of the most beautiful compensations of this life that no man can sincerely try to help another without helping himself.

— RALPH WALDO EMERSON

VALUE TIME

Time is your most precious gift because you only have a set amount of it. You can make more money, but you can't make more time. When you give someone your time, you are giving them a portion of your life that you'll never get back. Your time is your life. That is why the greatest gift you can give someone is your time.

— RICK WARREN

Our great object in time is not to waste our passions and gifts on the things external that we must leave behind, but that we cultivate within us all that we can carry into the eternal progress beyond.

— EDWARD BULWER-LYTTON

You rarely have time for everything you want in this life, so you need to make choices. And hopefully your choices can come from a deep sense of who you are.

— FRED ROGERS

SHARE YOURSELF WITH THOSE YOU LOVE

Smile each day for those you love.
Let them know by the brightness of your face
that you are happy they're in your life.

Touch each day those you love.
Hold them close, even if briefly.
The human touch is one of the
most comforting things in our world,
and one of the most reassuring.

Allow yourself to be vulnerable to those you love.
It is a most frightening experience to be without shields,
but it can also be the most wonderful thing in the world
to find another holds your spirit carefully within their heart.

Believe that you deserve those you love.
Your love is the most precious gift
that you can bestow on another human.
You deserve to be loved in return—
without constraints, without reserve.

Be honest with those you love.
Let them know how important they are in your life.
Take care that they never have to
guess at what you think and feel.

— BRENDA HAGER

BE IN THE PRESENT

When you're in the present moment, past and future fade away. There are no mental conditions for happiness. The simple pleasures of a sunrise or a sunset, the breeze on your face, a smile that seems to reach into every cell of your body, or a heartfelt conversation are always available. When you're able to let go of thinking and relax, the clouds part. You automatically become like a child again and feel the radiant joy of the inner sun. When that sun shines, you feel whole — a part of something that extends far beyond your separate self.... In the holy moments of presence, you feel a kind of solidarity with life that is the very essence of inner peace.

— JOAN BORYSENKO, PHD

Living in the present brings the one thing most people spend their lives striving to achieve: peace. Relaxing into the present moment puts you in the mental and physical state of calm, quiet, and tranquility and finally gets us off the here-but-gotta-get-there treadmill. If you are in the moment doing whatever you are doing, then there is no time to examine the gap between your expectation and the reality of how things are, or between where you are and where you think you should be. You are too busy being *in* the moment to *analyze* it and find fault with it.

— CHÉRIE CARTER-SCOTT, PHD

TO LIVE A SOULFUL LIFE IS TO...

LOVE AND HONOR YOURSELF

Promise yourself that you'll always remember what a special person you are ✦ That you'll hold on to your hopes and reach out for your stars ✦ That you'll live with happiness over the years and over the miles ✦ That you'll "remember when..." and you'll always "look forward to..." ✦ That you'll do the things you have always wanted to do ✦ That you'll cherish your dreams as treasures you have kept ✦ That you'll enjoy life day by day and step by step ✦ Promise yourself a life of love and joy and all your dreams come true.

— COLLIN MCCARTY

Love and accept yourself, no matter what it takes to come to that love. Love your body, mind, emotions, and spirit, whether they fit an ideal or not. Love your unique self. Love where you are now in your life and where you have been and where you are going.

— BETTYCLARE MOFFATT

MAY YOU HAVE
A SOULFUL LIFE

May you find serenity and tranquility in a world
you may not always understand. May the pain you
have known and the conflict you have experienced
give you the strength to walk through life facing
each new situation with courage and optimism.
Always know that there are those whose love and
understanding will always be there, even when you
feel most alone. May you discover enough goodness
in others to believe in a world of peace. May a kind
word, a reassuring touch, and a warm smile be yours
every day of your life, and may you give these gifts as
well as receive them. Remember the sunshine when
the storm seems unending. Teach love to those who
know hate, and let that love embrace you as you go
into the world.

May the teachings of those you admire become part of you, so that you may call upon them. Remember, those whose lives you have touched and who have touched yours are always a part of you, even if the encounters were less than you would have wished. It is the content of the encounter that is more important than its form. May you not become too concerned with material matters, but instead place immeasurable value on the goodness in your heart. Find time in each day to see beauty and love in the world around you. Realize that each person has limitless abilities, but each of us is different in our own way. What you may feel you lack in one regard may be more than compensated for in another. What you feel you lack in the present may become one of your strengths in the future. May you see your future as one filled with promise and possibility. Learn to view everything as a worthwhile experience. May you find enough inner strength to determine your own worth by yourself and not be dependent on another's judgment of your accomplishments. May you always feel loved.

— SANDRA STURTZ HAUSS

(Acknowledgments continued from page 4)

Rochelle Lynn Holt for "Take nothing for granted." Copyright © 2006 by Rochelle Lynn Holt. All rights reserved.

Rhena Schweitzer Miller and Newmarket Press for "What does the word 'soul' mean?" from THE WORDS OF ALBERT SCHWEITZER by Albert Schweitzer. Copyright © 2004 by Newmarket Press. All rights reserved.

Fireside Books, a division of Simon and Schuster, Inc., for "The spiritual dimension is your core…" from THE SEVEN HABITS OF HIGHLY EFFECTIVE PEOPLE by Stephen R. Covey. Copyright © 1989 by Stephen R. Covey. All rights reserved.

Heacock Literary Agency for "Live as well as you know…" from THE ART OF LIVING, DAY BY DAY by Wilferd A. Peterson, published by Simon & Schuster. Copyright © 1972 by Wilferd A. Peterson. All rights reserved.

Simon & Schuster Adult Publishing Group for "Go for a walk…" from WIN THE WEIGHT GAME by Sarah, The Duchess of York and Weight Watchers. Copyright © 2000 by The Duchess of York and Weight Watchers International, Inc. All rights reserved. And for "Love and accept…" from AN AUTHENTIC WOMAN: SOULWORK FOR THE WISDOM YEARS by BettyClare Moffatt. Copyright © 1999 by BettyClare Moffatt. All rights reserved.

Broadway Books, a division of Random House, Inc., for "Compassion is the act of opening…," "To live in a state of grace…," and "Living in the present…" from IF LIFE IS A GAME, THESE ARE THE RULES by Chérie Carter-Scott, PhD. Copyright © 1998 by Chérie Carter-Scott, PhD. All rights reserved.

Harcourt for "We do not exist for ourselves…" from NO MAN IS AN ISLAND by Thomas Merton. Copyright © 1955 by The Abbey of Our Lady of Gethsemani. Copyright renewed 1983 by the Trustees of the Merton Legacy Trust. All rights reserved.

Parallax Press for "Human beings are full of desires" from THE ENERGY OF PRAYER by Thich Nhat Hanh. Copyright © 2006 by United Buddhist Church. All rights reserved.

Harmony Books, a division of Random House, Inc., for "Simplicity is not a matter of time…" from A WOMAN'S GUIDE TO A SIMPLER LIFE by Andrea Van Steenhouse, PhD. Copyright © 1996 by Andrea Van Steenhouse, PhD and Doris A. Fuller. All rights reserved.

Ralph S. Marston, Jr., for "It's useful to get things done…" and "When you think you know it all…." Copyright © 2005, 2006 by Ralph S. Marston, Jr. Originally published in "The Daily Motivator" at www.dailymotivator.com. All rights reserved.

Crown Publishers, Inc., a division of Random House, Inc., for "We are too busy…" from 365 WAYS TO CHANGE YOUR LIFE by Suzanne Somers. Copyright © 1999 by Suzanne Somers. All rights reserved.

Hyperion for "Some days, doing 'the best we can'…" and "You rarely have time…" from THE WORLD ACCORDING TO MISTER ROGERS by Fred Rogers. Copyright © 2004 by Family Communications, Inc. Reprinted by permission of Hyperion. All rights reserved.

Jeremy P. Tarcher/Putnam, a division of Penguin Group (USA), Inc., for "Perfectionism is not a quest…" from THE ARTIST'S WAY: A SPIRITUAL PATH TO HIGHER CREATIVITY by Julia Cameron. Copyright © 1992 by Julia Cameron. All rights reserved.

Ocean Tree Books for "If you're harboring the slightest…" and "Inner peace comes through…" from PEACE PILGRIM: HER LIFE AND WORK IN HER OWN WORDS by Peace Pilgrim. Copyright © 1982, 1991 by Friends of Peace Pilgrim. All rights reserved.

Zondervan for "Resentment always hurts you…" and "Time is your most precious gift…" from THE PURPOSE DRIVEN LIFE by Rick Warren. Copyright © 2002 by Rick Warren. All rights reserved.

Little, Brown and Company for "If we don't forgive ourselves for…" by Joan Borysenko, PhD, and "You nourish your soul by…" by Rabbi Harold Kushner from HANDBOOK FOR THE SOUL by Richard Carlson and Benjamin Shield. Copyright © 1995 by Richard Carlson and Benjamin Shield. All rights reserved.

Gotham Books, a division of Penguin Group (USA), Inc., for "Living authentically is what you're doing…" from HARD QUESTIONS FOR AN AUTHENTIC LIFE by Susan Piver. Copyright © 2004 by Susan Piver. All rights reserved.

Pantheon Books, a division of Random House, Inc., for "When one is a stranger…" from GIFT FROM THE SEA by Anne Morrow Lindbergh. Copyright © 1955, 1975 by Anne Morrow Lindbergh. Copyright renewed 1983 by Anne Morrow Lindbergh. All rights reserved.

Marie Beynon Ray for "I have never known an 'interesting' person…" from HOW NEVER TO BE TIRED, published by The Bobbs-Merrill Company. Copyright © 1938, 1944 by Marie Beynon Ray. All rights reserved.

Rachel Snyder for "Sometimes you're just done…." Copyright © 2006 by Rachel Snyder. All rights reserved.

Hay House, Inc., Carlsbad, CA, for "When you're in the present…" from INNER PEACE FOR BEAUTIFUL PEOPLE by Joan Borysenko, PhD. Copyright © 2001 by Joan Borysenko. All rights reserved.

Brenda Hager for "Smile each day…." Copyright © 2006 by Brenda Hager. All rights reserved.

A careful effort has been made to trace the ownership of selections used in this anthology in order to obtain permission to reprint copyrighted material and give proper credit to the copyright owners. If any error or omission has occurred, it is completely inadvertent, and we would like to make corrections in future editions provided that written notification is made to the publisher:

BLUE MOUNTAIN ARTS, INC., P.O. Box 4549, Boulder, Colorado 80306.